connections

RENEÉ ROSEN – A Retrospective

To Nadine + Scott
Stel Connected !
Renée Rosen

Requests for permission to reprint, in whole or in part, should be addressed to:
Renee Rosen, 11 Riverside Drive, New York, New York, 10023, USA.

ISBN 978-1-60585-282-9

All measurements in inches unless otherwise noted.
Book Design by Gerard Babakian

Printed and bound in Canada by Art Bookbindery

For Marty, for his loving support

and encouragement every step of the way.

ACKNOWLEDGMENTS

Without the help of family and friends this book would never have been possible. I give my deepest thanks to my son Josh, whose spirit and creative inquisitiveness push me to find new answers; to my daughter Beth, who discovered ways to become a new woman, which inspired many paintings; to my in-law children, John Buell and Sue Kalt, for their consistent enthusiasm; to my sister Mili Klein and her daughter Mindia, for their love, encouragement and real help; to all of my grandchildren, Joelle, Sasha, Maya, Sylvie, and Jacob, for helping me see the world with fresh eyes.

This book would not have come about without the untiring devotion of my editor, Maria Weisbin. Special thanks also go to Jim Weisbin, Wendy Panken, Gerard Babakian and Phyllis Hunt for coming through when things were tough, and to my dear late friend, Robin Hess who so much wanted to see this book completed.

And to the Puffin Foundation for their grant.

CONTENTS

FOREWORD

Growing up with art has been an extraordinary privilege. Along with the usual assortment of children's toys, my brother and I were surrounded by beautiful, thought provoking paintings that became our familiar friends. My mother taught us to open our eyes to the world, visually and politically. A walk to the park was an opportunity to see the beauty in the smallest flower, in the shape of a branch, in the color of the sky, or in the texture of a tree trunk. She taught us to look at the world with strong clear eyes, to see both its beauty and its challenges. We learned early that my mother was equally passionate about art and social justice. She was on the frontline in school reform; she marched for civil rights and integration; she led consciousness-raising groups during the feminist movement, and protested against the Vietnam War, with us, her children, in tow.

Renée uses paint to express her vision of the world. Her passion for social justice and beauty go hand in hand, creating an art that reflects both her aesthetic and her deep feelings about the world. Her paintings are magical: colors, forms, lines, and shapes dance musically together expressing original ideas. Her series paintings create variations on a theme, suggesting many interpretations.

Throughout my life I have witnessed her creative spirit unfolding in her work and seen her persevere, fighting to overcome the obstacles that so many artists face in a culture that undervalues art. She had the unwavering love and support of my father, Marty, who admired her and valued her work beyond words. Renee's deep respect for art and creativity supported my own creative work and that of my brother Josh, for which we are forever grateful.

It is with pride and joy that I introduce this collection of paintings, the life's work of a painter whose life and work both continue to grow.

Beth Rosen
New Haven, 2007

INTRODUCTION

I was born into a family whose roots dug deep into the working class Russian soil. Like many others who immigrated in the early 1900s, my family sought freedom to carry on their Jewish traditions and to escape the poverty they faced daily. America promised both. My parents shared the struggle for freedom and equality with neighbors who came from the same beginnings. My house became a center for meetings organized to make the life of the working-class better. As a young child, I became aware of their concerns while I sat at the kitchen table playing with pencil and paper as my mother and her friends talked over coffee. My mind slipped into blank space amidst the buzzing of voices, the aroma of chicken soup cooking on the stove and the play of light coming in through the curtained kitchen window. First I scribbled and doodled, then I deliberately worked for different effects, fine feather strokes, curlicues and zigzags. Pencil and paper was all that was available, but it was enough to satisfy my need.

Later, in elementary school, my eyes often followed the line of a classmate's profile. Sometimes it took the teacher's ruler coming down hard on my hand to bring me back to what she was saying. It soon became obvious to my family that I needed someplace to play with art. They enrolled me in children's art classes at the Brooklyn Museum. In high school I always chose art classes for my electives. My teachers encouraged me to apply for a scholarship with the National Academy of Fine Arts, which I was awarded. I studied sculpture with Chaim Gross, painting with the three Soyer brothers, at the Henry Street Settlement, and drawing at the Art Student's League. And so, almost without realizing it, I embarked on a life-long journey into the world of fine art.

Then, for a time, college, marriage, family and community affairs pushed art out; it seemed irrelevant. But I couldn't push it entirely out of my mind. I always managed to find a corner for a makeshift studio where I could draw or paint once in a while. Finally, I decided to take my art seriously and enrolled as a full-time student at the Brooklyn Museum Art School. Here I began to absorb the prevailing aesthetic. I immersed myself in current ideas about line, color and form. I found creating paintings that were then called "art for art's sake," a wonderfully liberating experience. However, it separated me from the rest of my life. I needed to carry my history and my involvement in current events into my art. I had to create paintings that continued to explore aesthetic possibilities speaking of our time in history. It has been a difficult and rewarding journey.

Renée Rosen
New York City, 2008

EARLY WORK

LANDSCAPE AND
STILL LIFE PAINTINGS

Seeing art as a purely visual statement concerned with qualities on the surface – brush stroke, color, nuance and composition – was considered the supreme mode of expression when I entered the art world. My high regard for women artists who were immersed in abstract expressionism, such as Elaine DeKooning and Helen Frankenthaler, led me to paint that way. But I soon found that for me abstraction was vacuous. I turned to other ways. Using figurative or landscape images I searched for meaningful form.

Airscape — Oil on canvas 62x40

Whose Land — Oil on canvas 14x13

The Monolith — Oil on canvas 22x28

Marty's Landscape — Oil on canvas 22x25

The Birdcage —
Oil on canvas 8x10

Sunshine Umbrella —
Oil on canvas 15x24

My interest in composition and how I could manage the space in terms of form led to a short-lived experiment with still life.

I was struck by the atmosphere in the elevator that I rode every day, and began to see people as still lives. Everyone was silent, leaning against the walls – so still. And then came the Vietnam War and I saw still life differently. I saw those lives stilled.

The Elevator – Oil on canvas 30x40

Conformity –
Oil on canvas 24x36

The Crowd – Oil on canvas 22x40

Still Life – Oil on canvas 40x50

Singers – Oil and pen and ink on canvas 24x24

Lovers – Oil on canvas 24x36

Crossings – Oil on canvas 62x40

WOMAN'S INNER SEARCH

Betty Friedan's book *The Feminine Mystique* reawakened lessons I had learned in my mother's kitchen, but other questions that I had not confronted before began to haunt me. This body of work emerged as a result.

The Beginning – Oil on canvas 22x28

What Else? – Oil on canvas 12x18

Coffee – Oil on canvas 12x14

**Mirror, Mirror
On The Wall** —
Oil on canvas 19x24

Three Passages —
Oil on canvas 20x28

Reject – Oil on canvas 19x24

Time Passes –
Oil on canvas 19x22

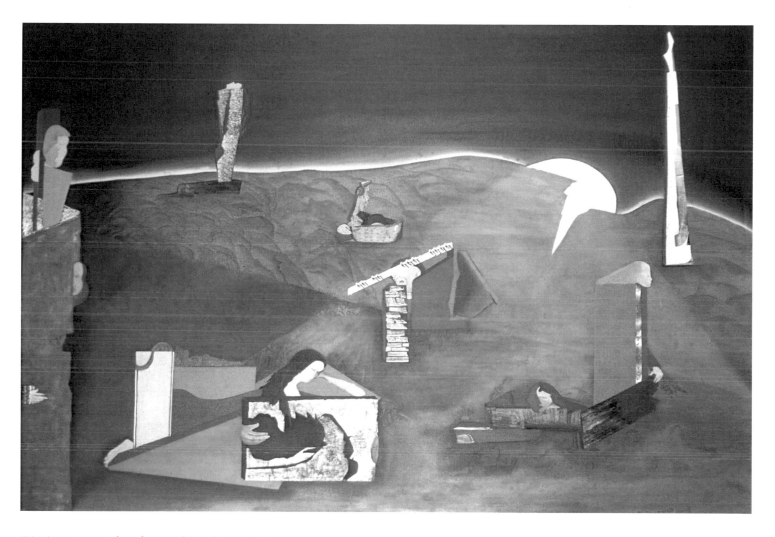

Fitting In – Oil and Mixed Media 40x52

MID-CAREER WORK

LIFE'S MAGIC

Many questions arose as I looked at the night sky – what is beyond what I can see or comprehend? Is it all chance that you and I are here, on this little spot on earth, at the same time? Would a few seconds in time have changed everything? Do we have any control when confronting the big questions? And what happens when it's all over? Are we living in a science fiction story?

Inner Space – Oil on canvas 30x48

Crystal Ball – Oil on canvas 12x14

Looking Beyond — Oil on canvas 16x24

Choices — Oil and Mixed Media 30x48

Mixing It Up – Oil on canvas 30x48

Passing Through – Oil on canvas 36x50

Where Are We Going – Oil on canvas 30x48

CONCIOUSNESS IV

In the early seventies, at the time the feminists were already gathering to formulate the Equal Rights Amendment, Charles Reich published *The Greening of America*. It purported to outline the forces responsible for creating our country's national character. He named and described three major forces, each resulting in a new and more evolved level of consciousness, Consciousness I, II and III. In consciousness III he postulated that our society viewed most worthy those who were able to transcend their limitations to achieve personal liberation. Nowhere in the book does he mention women or the particular challenges they face in their struggle for cultural and legal equality. I saw this exclusion as a glaring injustice and so created the following body of work, which I called Consciousness IV.

Consciousness IV – Oil on canvas 40x52

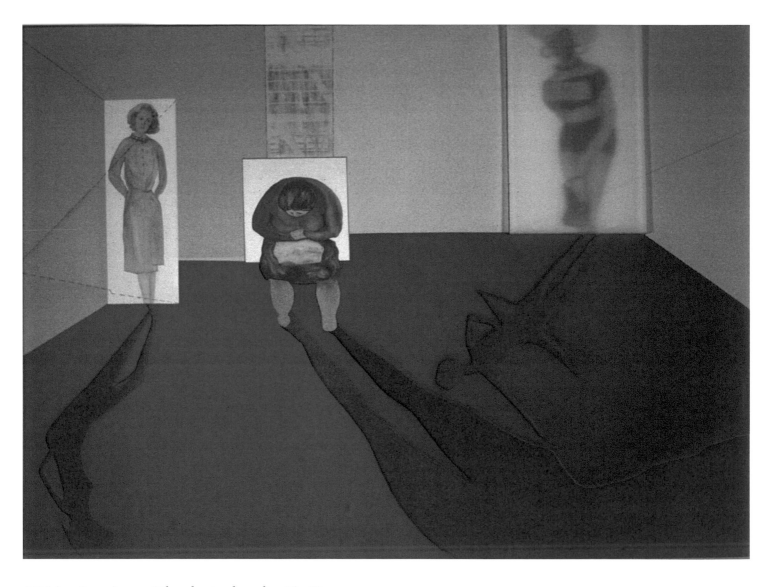

Hidden Longings– Oil and mixed media 52x40

Strange Landscape – Oil on canvas 60x40

Transitions – Oil and mixed media 50x50

MULTIPLE PERSPECTIVES

Newspapers. Magazines. Photos. Images everywhere. Advertisements on lamp posts, subways and buses, even on cereal boxes, divert the eye. Television, computer screens, store windows; pictures, pictures everyplace. As I walk down the street one image mixes with another. Each one stays in my mind's eye overlapping for a moment with the next one. I decided to use this experience by cutting pictures into strips and interweaving them, creating a whole more telling than its parts. Up close one picture is visible. Stand back and others come together. Look deeply and there's a message there. Just like life.

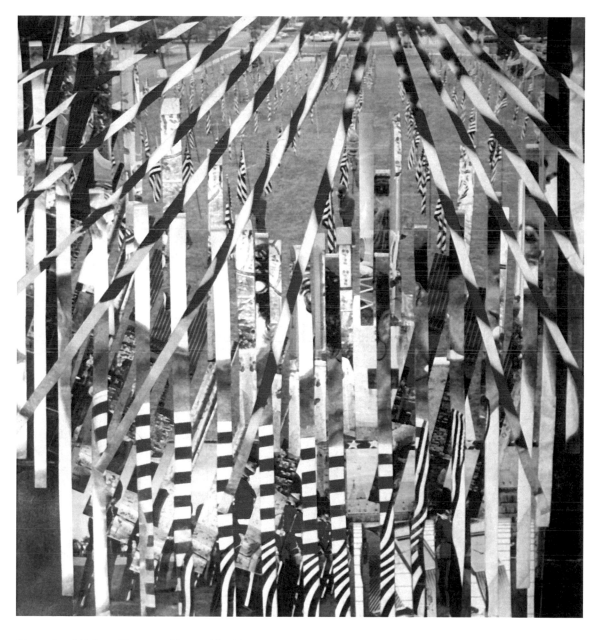

Fourth of July – Paper collage 15x15

Nature's Bounty – Paper collage 13x16

Water Plus – Paper collage 18x24

Romance – Paper collage 12x15

Duck Soup– Paper collage 18x30

I felt the need to introduce an abstract element that could intensify the emotional aspect underlying the collaged pictures. Combining realism with abstraction was something I was always interested in. After all, isn't that what we see in life all the time?

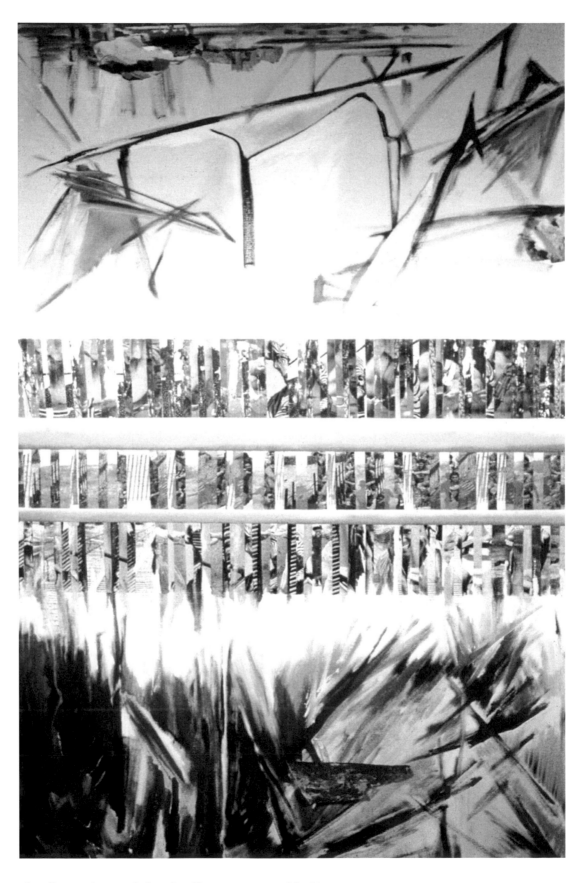

Conflagration — Oil and collage on canvas 30x54

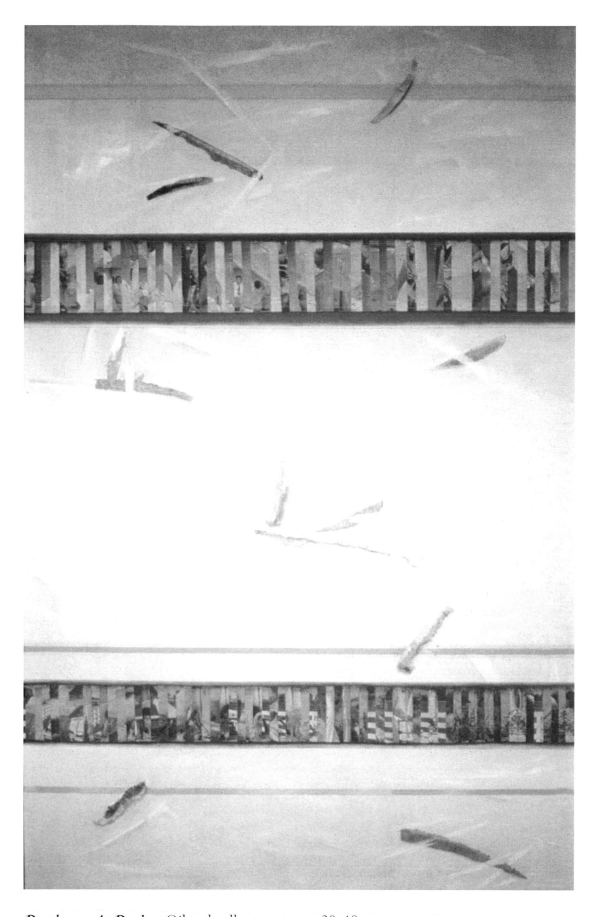

Daydream At Dusk – Oil and collage on canvas 30x48

Taking Off – Oil and collage on canvas 30x54

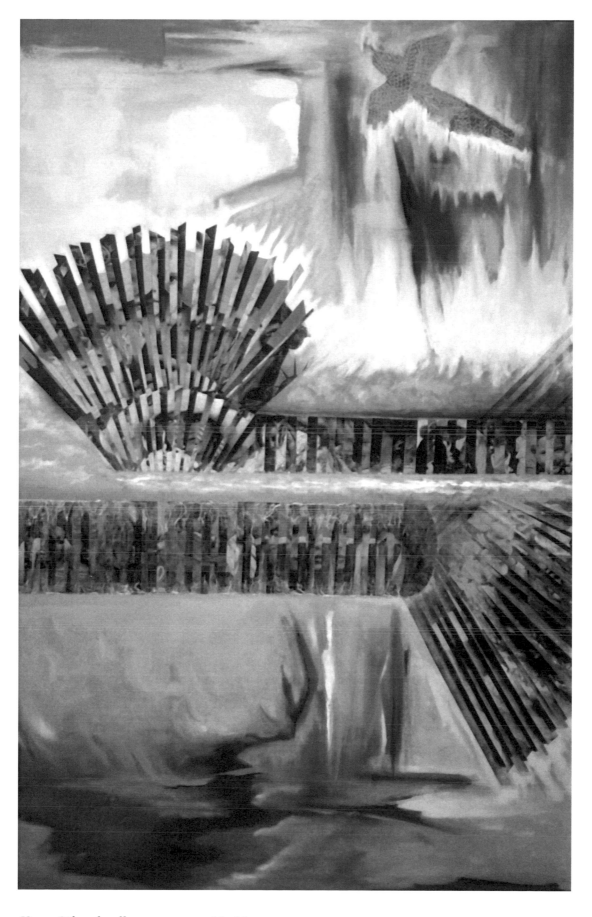

She – Oil and collage on canvas 30x48

MONOPRINTS

Making monoprints was a needed relief from the collage work I had been totally consumed by. I came up with a way to do a handprint and then overlay it with pastels to add color. It was so much fun to do these that after pulling some thirty prints I had to force myself to stop.

Untitled #1– Monoprint on paper 18x24

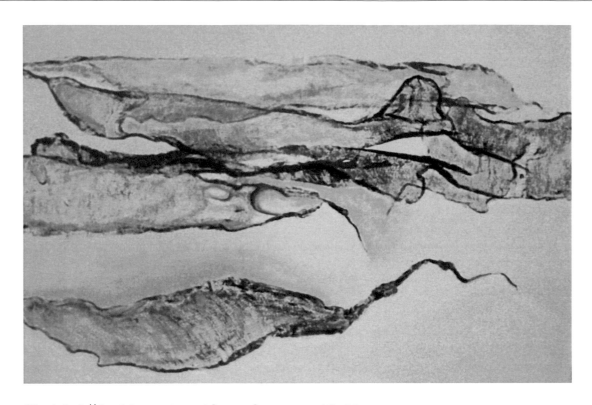

Untitled #2 – Monoprint with pastel on paper 18x24

Untitled #3 –
Monoprint with pastel on paper
18x24

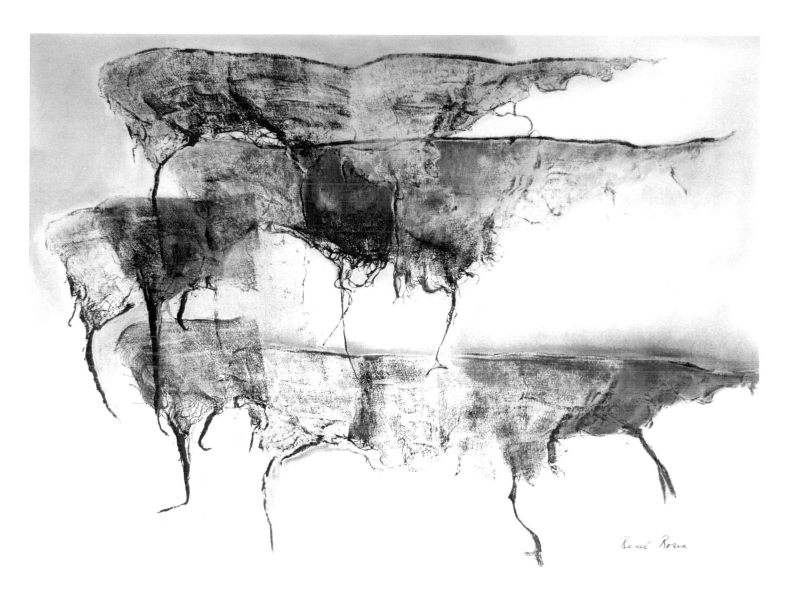

Untitled #5 – Monoprint with pastel on paper 18x24

MONOPRINTS — GOING FURTHER

The smell of oil paints had for too long been absent from my studio, but I wasn't ready to give up the joy of making monoprints. So I found a way to combine the two. I quickly saw that once again I needed to express ideas about the human condition.

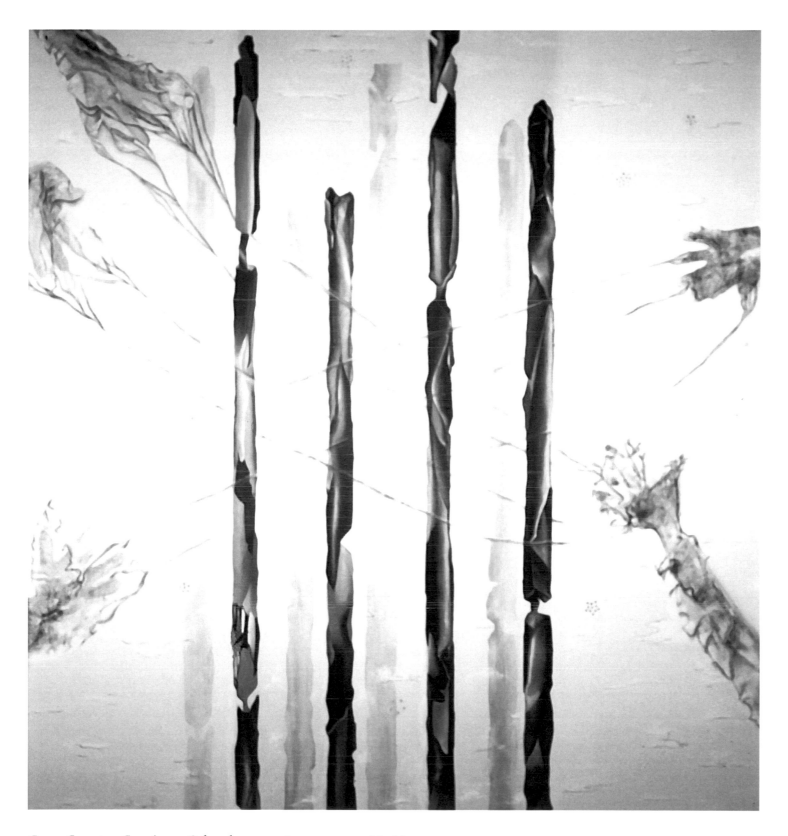

Cross Country Cousins – Oil and monoprint on canvas 54x48

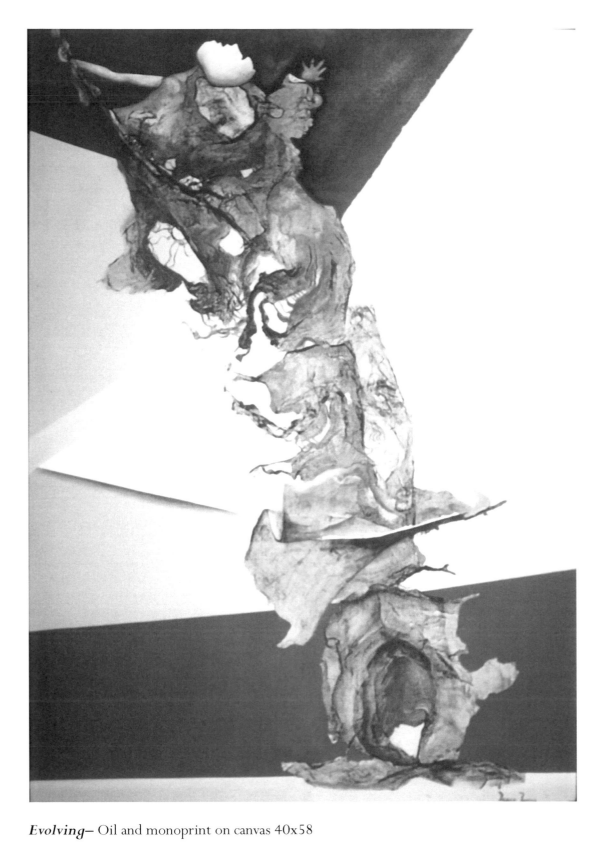

Evolving– Oil and monoprint on canvas 40x58

Waiting – Oil and monoprint on canvas 46x48

Nostalgia – Oil and monoprint on canvas 14x25

Watch Out –
Oil on monoprint on canvas
24x28

The Rising Sun – Oil and monoprint on canvas 24x34

SINGULAR IDEAS

A group of artists from Women Caucus for Art decided to do a group project called "The Puzzle Project." Each artist was to do a painting shaped as a puzzle piece. We thought they would all fit together as a picture puzzle, but that never came about. We did show them as individual paintings over the course of time in several venues. Later I added the two side panels, in my mind completing the picture.

The paintings in the following section are not part of a series. Each was done because of a singular idea, or to experiment with a different medium.

Enigmatic Sphere – The Puzzle Project – Oil and collage on canvas 5 ft. x 10 ft.

The Lesson – Oil and collage on canvas 33x46

Parade – Oil and collage on canvas 30x36

Bull – Oil and collage on canvas 30x42

Illusions – Oil and collage on canvas 54x46

LATER WORK

THE GODDESS SERIES

I have always been entranced by changing shapes; how the lines, forms and colors melt into each other and then move away; soft wind blowing on water, shifting cloud formations. The curved flow of the river, the softness of the clouds, the colors of flowers; are these aspects of nature's female side? Perhaps everything on earth has a gender, even everything we create. My attempt here was to capture this female essence in particular locations. I call this series Goddess.

Seattle Goddess – Oil and collage on canvas 24x48

San Francisco Goddess – Oil and collage on canvas 40x50

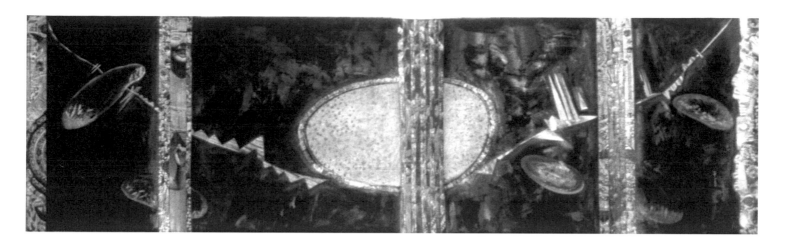

Manhattan Goddess – Oil and collage on canvas 48x15

Santa Fe Goddess – Oil and collage on canvas 28x54

Cape Cod Goddess – Oil and collage on canvas 34x40

Anchorage Goddess – Oil and collage on canvas 40x50

Virginia Goddess – Oil and collage on canvas 20x30

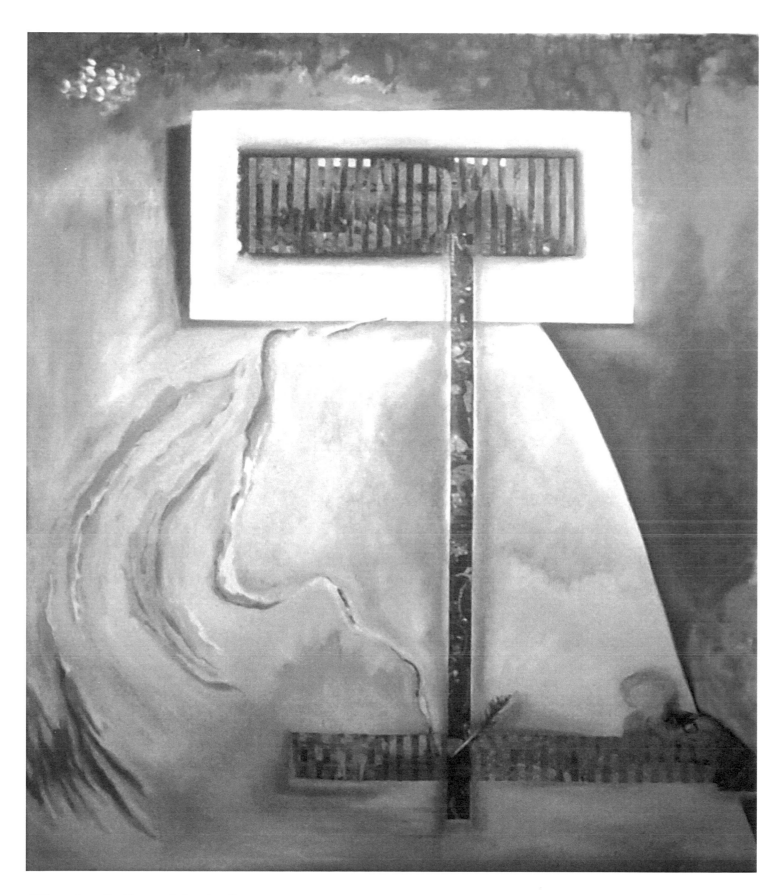

Milwaukee Goddess – Oil and collage on canvas 40x48

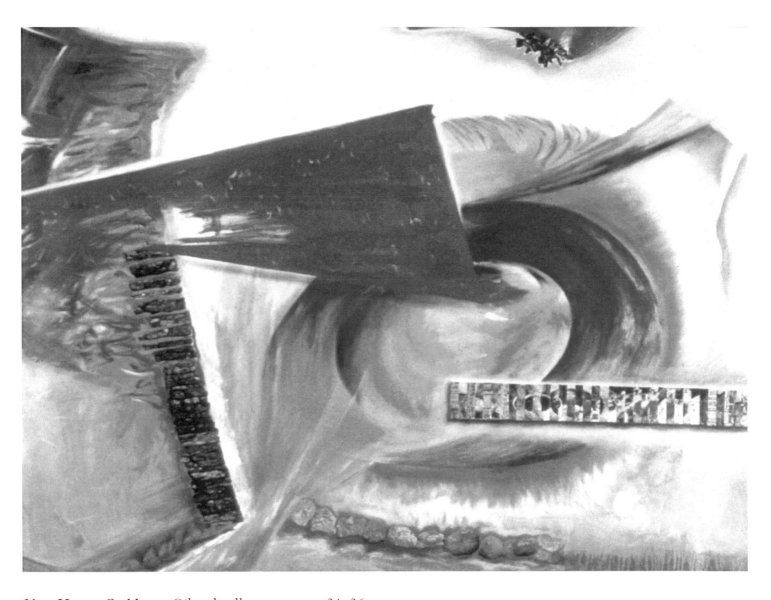

New Haven Goddess – Oil and collage on canvas 34x36

Newport Goddess – Oil and collage on canvas 24x26

Maine Goddess – Oil and collage on canvas 19x23

Kansas Goddess – Oil and collage on canvas 24x40

Chicago Goddess – Oil and collage on canvas 25x40

WINDOWS

I spent a lot of time looking out of my studio window. I saw people walking, trees and houses, high and low. I saw forms so crowded together that they were indistinguishable. Crunched shapes, gray and brown, turned out to be refuse left on the broken street below. I saw the connection of all the forms, lines and colors. To see what is there, and what is not easily visible is a lifetime job. I used the shape of my window as the shape of my canvas and the window as a metaphor for the world outside.

Connections – Oil and collage on canvas 35x72

The Shining Light – Oil and collage on canvas 35x72

Over The Mountain I Saw Her – Oil and collage on canvas 35x72

Halleluliah! A Birth – Oil and collage on canvas 35x72

On The Edge – Oil and collage on canvas 35x72

Oh! Joy, Spring Is Here – Oil and collage on canvas 35x72

Time Is A Snake In The Grass – Oil and collage on canvas 35x72

BLACK AND WHITE
AND RED (READ) ALL OVER

What is black and white and red all over? A newspaper. I have been puzzling over another aspect of the old riddle. Namely, what effect does the daily invasion of newspapers have on our lives? Does it in some subtle way change our view of the world? Perhaps by combining certain articles on the same page, a subliminal message is transmitted. On what basis is one picture chosen over another? Do the papers harp on selected topics, and does that over time influence our concepts? What about the lost information – the stories and pictures they do not print – how does that alter what we do see? Does the order and design of the page inform our aesthetic and moral judgment?

Where Shall We Go – Oil and collage on canvas 41x37

Interruption II – Oil and collage on canvas 40x30

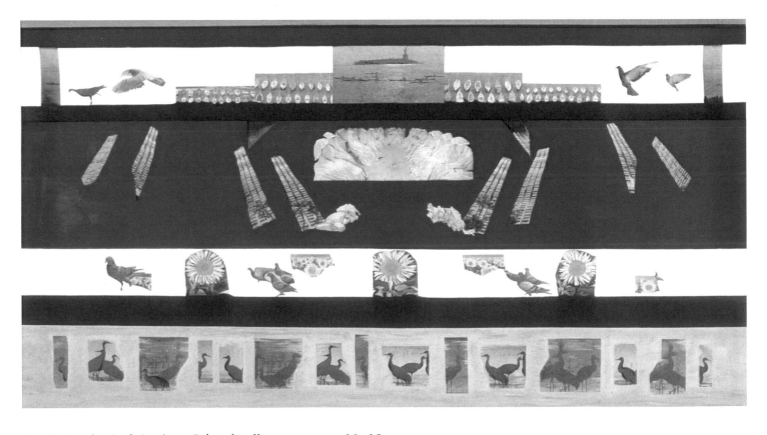

Say It Again And Again – Oil and collage on canvas 39x25

Wave The Flag – Oil and collage on canvas 35x33

Regimentation – Oil and collage on canvas 28x52

Interruption I – Oil and collage on canvas 22x20

Hole In One – Oil and collage on canvas 24x19

Contradiction – Oil and collage on canvas 25x40

Smoke – Oil and collage on canvas 37x45

Whitewashed – Oil and collage on canvas 20x36

Morning Service – Oil and collage on canvas 40x38

Dead Words – Oil and collage on canvas 50x60

Jump For Joy – Oil and collage on canvas 45x37

With Your Morning Coffee – Oil and collage on canvas 45x37

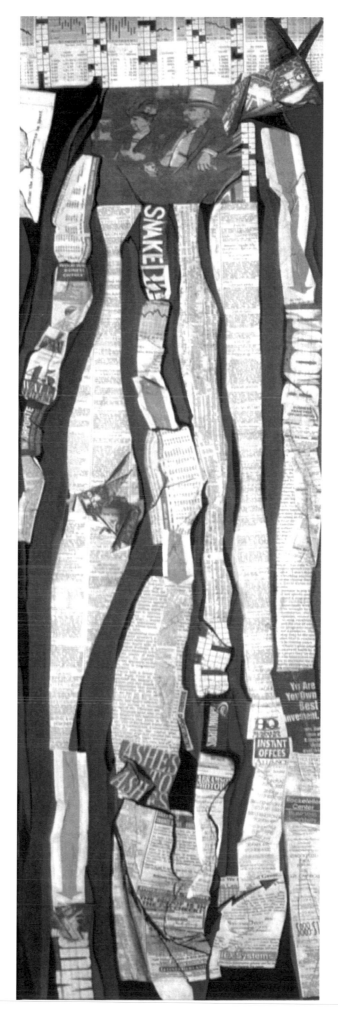

Snake– Oil and collage on canvas 37x10

PASSING ON — CHOICES

"The most beautiful thing we can experience is the mysterious," Albert Einstein said. His words seem incomprehensible when confronting issues of mortality. To see beauty in death escaped me. Then it became clear to me that remembered experiences are segments of time and that these segments move like waves of the ocean. They are always changing as they move forward.

Timeline– Oil and collage 12x36

Go With The Flow – Oil and collage on canvas 50x40

Washed Ashore – Oil and collage on canvas 50x50

What Remains – Oil and collage on canvas 50x60

As a relief from the serious work I was involved in, I sat with a blank mind, doodling. The pen in my hand brought me back to my early days of playing with a pencil. It felt good to relax and let my hand sweep across the paper. Then came color and the satisfaction of producing these pictures.

Untitled 108 – Pen and ink with pastel 7.5x9.5

Untitled 106 –
Pen and ink with pastel
7.5x9.5

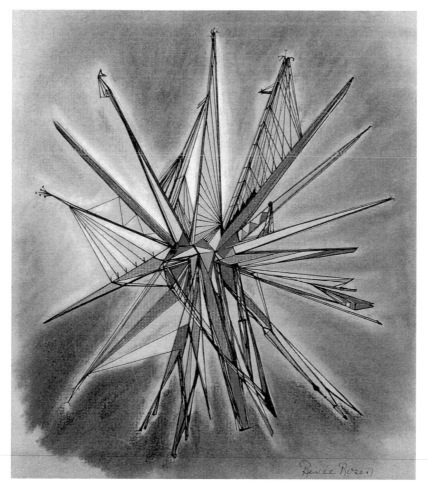

Untitled 109 –
Pen and ink with pastel
7.5x9.5

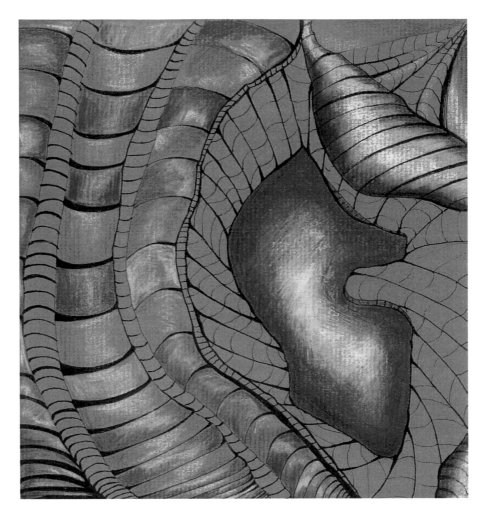

Untitled 110 – Pen and ink with pastel 7.5x9.5

Untitled 107 – Pen and ink with pastel 7.5x9.5

After working through troubling questions of mortality in the Passing On series and finding relief in the ink and pastel drawings, I recognized that though we may not be able to choose the road we must travel, sometimes in life we have a choice in how we look at that road.

Light And Dark — Oil and collage on canvas 49x34

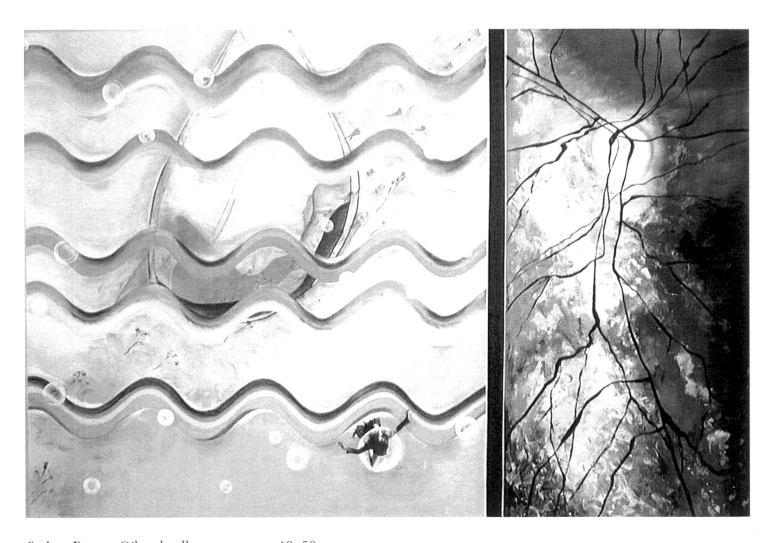

Swing Free – Oil and collage on canvas 40x50

Twist And Turn – Oil and collage 49x34

AMERICAN PORTRAITS

As a child, I drew the profiles of my classmates because that was all I could see from my seat. Later, in art school, I sketched faces but the models' bodies interested me more. I carried a sketchbook in the subways and sketched as I rode back and forth from school or work. But I never thought seriously about straightforward portraiture until I took notice of a teenage girl's offbeat clothing. She seemed so free, so original. I was intrigued and looked further. In some faces I saw confusion or conflict. Some people seemed not sure who they were anymore – their roots in conflict with America's expectations. I wanted to capture American faces in the context of America's vision of them.

Breaking Out – Oil and collage on canvas 28x34

Looking Back – Oil and collage on canvas 28x34

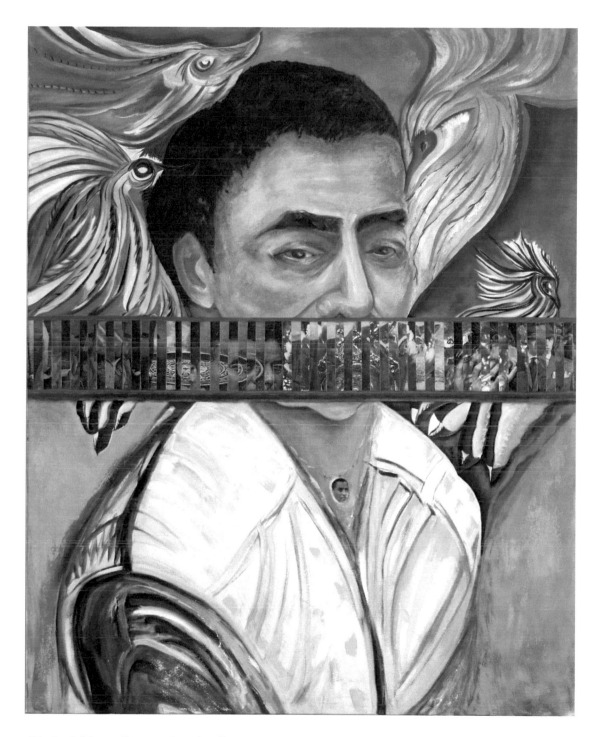

Birds Of Paradise – Oil and collage on canvas 28x34

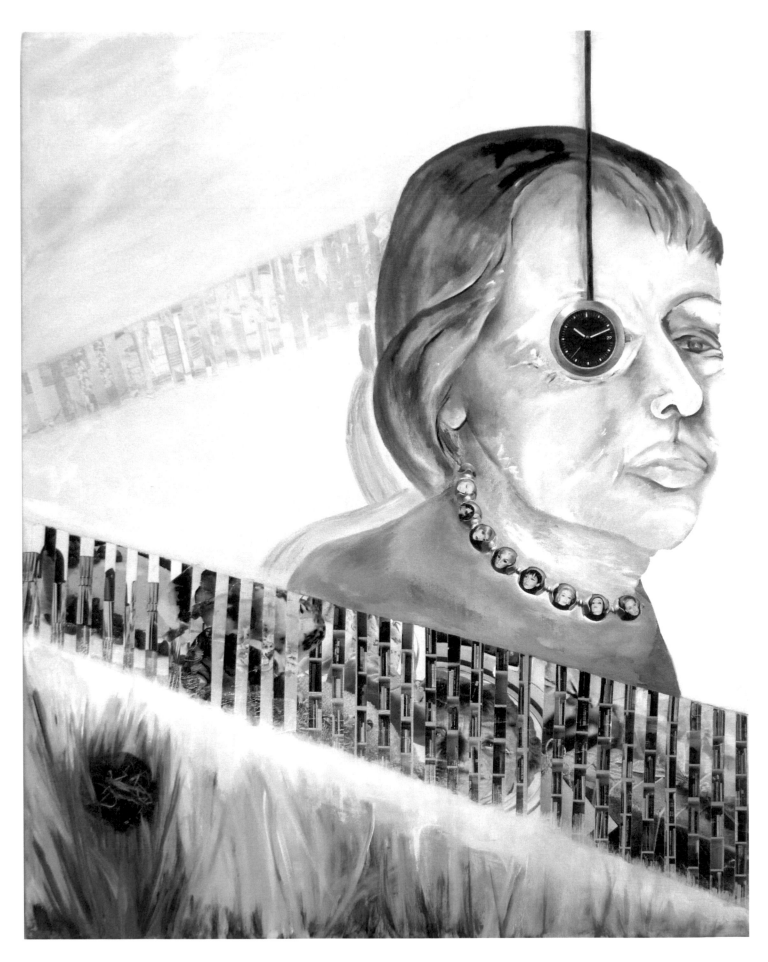

The Ticking Clock – Oil and collage on canvas 24x30

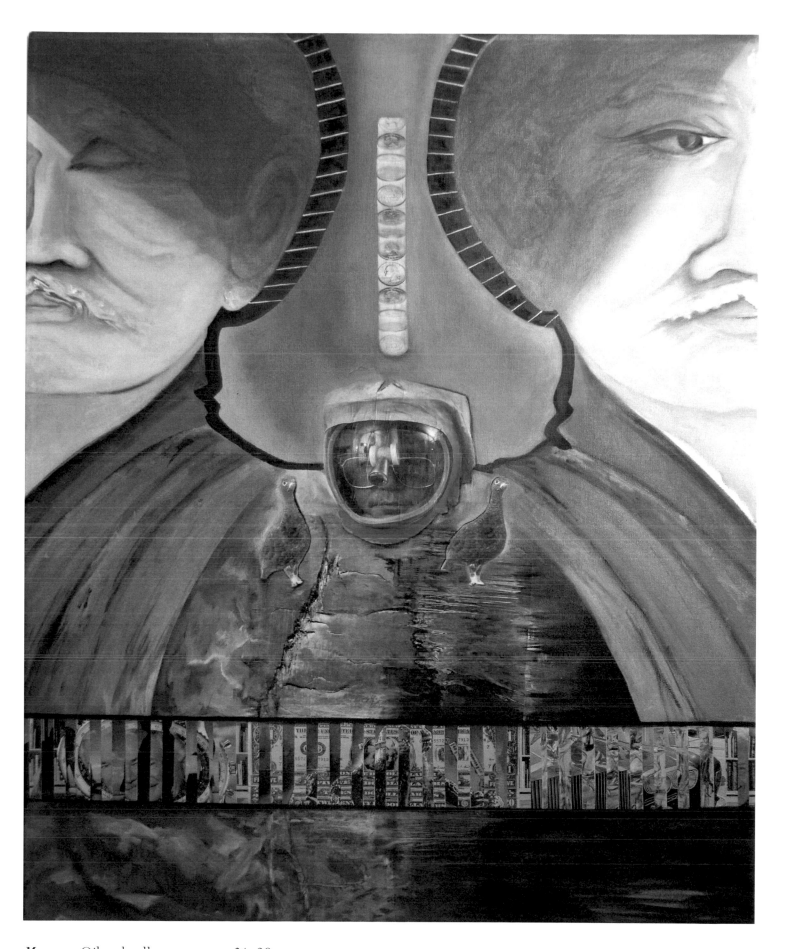

Money – Oil and collage on canvas 24x30

The Children – Oil and collage on canvas 22x38

The Illegal Immigrant – Oil and collage on canvas 26x38

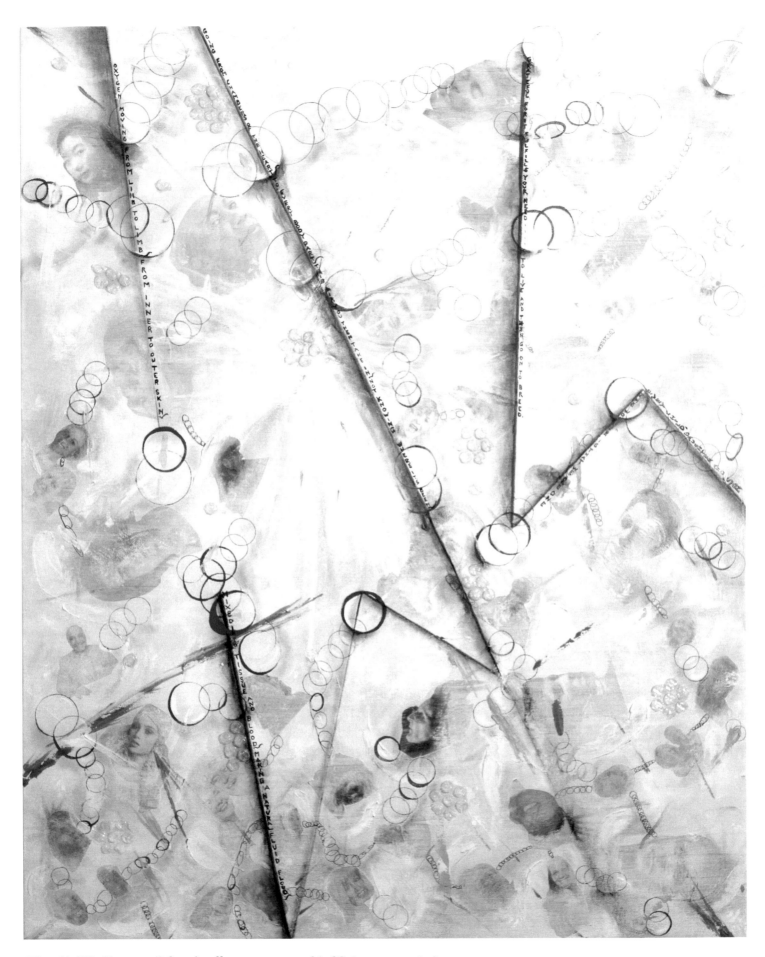

The Air We Share – Oil and collage on canvas 24x30 (text opposite)

THE AIR WE SHARE

Oxygen moving from limb to limb
from inner to outer skin
mixed into tissue and blood
making a natural fluid flood.

Going from chambers of the heart
to every body part
this air you then take in
not knowing where it's been.

Grateful for it fulfills your need
to love and go on to breed.
The wonder is that we are one,
every child, daughter and son.

— For Bessie

AFTERWORD

I remember running my finger over a bump on my bedroom wall and noticing how that little protrusion cast a shadow and how that shadow changed as the light in the room changed. I soon realized that before I could draw or paint, I had to learn to see. I started to look at artists' pictures to discover how they saw. In a children's class at the Brooklyn Museum, I studied by copying from the masters. My first book of art, given to me on my sixteenth birthday, was a collection of the paintings of Vincent van Gogh. Every time I turned the page, which I did over and over again, I lost my breath. His expressive brush strokes, bold color and sensitive line astonished me. I owe a debt of gratitude for the insights and passion of too many artists to mention here. But I must mention Picasso's horror of war "Guernica", Magritte's satirical expressions, Nevelson's determination, Pollack's liberation, and Judy Chicago's homage to women and to craft.

I believe people will always make art. The need to express one's interpretation of life, and of aesthetics exists in all of us and some, I hope, will devote the major part of their lives to it.